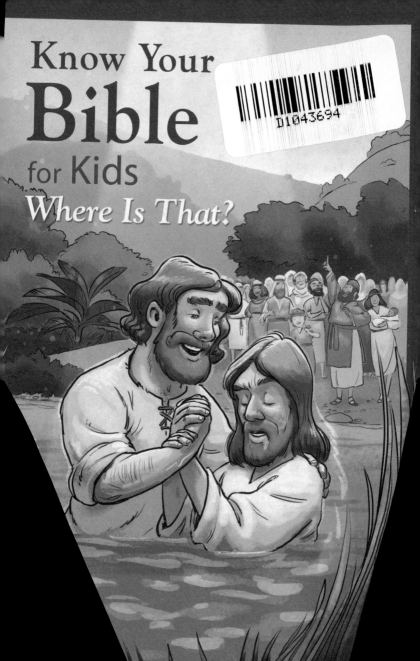

Know Your
Bible
for Kids
Where Is That?

Know Your
Bible
for Kids
Where Is That?

Donna K. Maltese

Illustrated by David Miles

BARBOUR BOOKS
An Imprint of Barbour Publishing, Inc.

Published by Barbour Books, an imprint of Barbour Publishing, Inc., P.O. Box 719, Uhrichsville, Ohio 44683 www.barbourbooks.com

Our mission is to publish and distribute inspirational products offering exceptional value and biblical encouragement to the masses.

Printed in the United States of America.

04860 1114 VP

Contents

Introduction

From the book of Genesis to the book of Revelation, the Bible is filled with hundreds of captivating stories. And starring in these many stories are more than 3,000 different people. But sometimes just as important as these people are the more than 1,000 settings in which their stories take place. In this unique book, *Know Your Bible for Kids—Where Is That?*, we have chosen 99 of the most interesting and important places in scripture. Every fascinating and illustrated sketch—from the miraculous water pile-up in the town of Adam to the never-ending flour and oil in the village of Zarephath—follows this outline:

- *Where is this place?* A brief geographic description of the site mentioned in the Bible.
- *What's it all about?* Details about what happened there.
- *What's an important verse about this place?* A key Bible verse about that site.
- *What does that mean to me?* What the history of this place teaches God's readers.

One of the great things about the Bible is the fact that we can learn so much about what happened where and with whom. As we imagine ourselves in each setting—even though it may still be shrouded in mystery or be in ruins today—that unique place, its history, its heroes, and God Himself come alive.

We hope you will use this fun, fascinating, and fact-filled book to better understand God's timeless lessons and realize that no matter where you are, God is always with you, guiding you today and into tomorrow.

Adam

Where is Adam?

This city was on the Jordan River.

What's it all about?

Joshua and the Israelites were trying to get into the land God had promised them. But first they had to cross the overflowing Jordan. The Lord told them that as soon as the priests carrying the Ark of God stepped into the river, the water would back up at the city of Adam and the people could cross.

What's an important verse about Adam?

Right away the water that was coming down the river stopped flowing. It piled up far away at a town called Adam near Zarethan. . . . So the people went across the Jordan River opposite Jericho.
JOSHUA 3:16 NIrV

What does that mean to me?

God will do amazing things to get you where He wants you to be.

Ai

Where is Ai?

Near the town of Jericho.

What's it all about?

The first time Joshua and the Israelites attacked this small village of Ai, they lost the battle. That's because after their earlier victory over Jericho, an Israelite named Achan had taken things that didn't belong to him. When Achan came clean with what he'd done, God gave Joshua a new battle plan and a promise.

What's an important verse about Ai?

"Do not be afraid or discouraged. Take all your fighting men and attack Ai, for I have given you the king of Ai, his people, his town, and his land."
JOSHUA 8:1 NLT

What does that mean to me?

When you obey God, He is sure to help you win over your enemies.

Aijalon

Where is Aijalon?

On the boundary between the kingdoms of Judah and Israel.

What's it all about?

Joshua and the Israelites fought five kings and their armies who wanted to take over the town of Gibeon. To totally defeat his enemies, Joshua asked God to make the sun and moon stand still, giving him enough light to finish the job.

What's an important verse about Aijalon?

"Sun, stand still over Gibeon. Moon, stand still over the Valley of Aijalon." So the sun stood still. The moon stopped. They didn't move again until the nation won the battle over its enemies.
JOSHUA 10:12–13 NIrV

What does that mean to me?

When you are working for God, He will listen to your prayers and move heaven and earth to help you.

Anab

Where is Anab?

In the mountains of Judah.

What's it all about?

Joshua and his great army fought many battles to win the Promised Land. During one of these fights, Joshua met up with a fierce race of giants.

What's an important verse about Anab?

Joshua went and killed the big powerful men in the hill country. He killed them in Hebron, Debir, Anab, and all the hill country of Judah and Israel.
JOSHUA 11:21 NLV

What does that mean to me?

God is big and mighty. He can take care of any giants you meet up with in life.

Antioch

Where is Antioch?

There are two places called Antioch. One is in Syria; the other was in Pisidia, the area of today's Turkey.

What's it all about?

In Antioch, Syria, Jews let non-Jews into their church. In Antioch, Pisidia, Paul and Barnabas did a great job in telling the people about Jesus. But some people weren't happy about that, so Paul and Barnabas left the city.

What's an important verse about Antioch, Syria?

Many people put their trust in the Lord and turned to Him . . . . For a year they [Paul and Barnabas] taught many people in the church. The followers were first called Christians in Antioch [Syria].
ACTS 11:21, 26 NLV

What's an important verse about Antioch, Pisidia?

They worked against Paul and Barnabas and made them leave their city. But Paul and Barnabas shook the dust off from their feet against them [in Antioch, Pisidia] and went to the city of Iconium.
ACTS 13:50–51 NLV

What does that mean to me?

When you are working for God, He finds a way to help you shake off defeat and live in victory!

Aphek

Where is Aphek?

Near Jezreel in Israel.

What's it all about?

The Israelites were not obeying God very well. So they lost a battle with the Philistines. Afterward, the Israelites decided to take the Ark of God (which had the 10 Commandments in it) with its priests—Hophni and Phinehas—into the next battle. The Israelites thought it would help them win. It didn't. They lost the battle–*and more!*

What's an important verse about Aphek?

The Israelite army was camped near Ebenezer, and the Philistines were at Aphek. . . . The Ark of God was captured, and Hophni and Phinehas, the two sons of Eli, were killed.
1 SAMUEL 4:1, 11 NLT

What does that mean to me?

Things won't save you—but being right with God will!

Armageddon

Where is Armageddon?

A word that shows up only one time in the Bible, *Armageddon* means "the Mount of Megiddo." It could be a real place or just a word being used to describe a battlefield.

What's it all about?

Armageddon is where a final battle will be fought between Christ and all the wicked people on earth. Christ will win!

What's an important verse about Armageddon?

Then the evil spirits gathered the kings together. The place where the kings met is called Armageddon in the Hebrew language.
REVELATION 16:16 NIrV

What does that mean to me?

Nothing is stronger or more powerful than Jesus Christ. When you are on His side, you will always come out a winner!

Ashdod

Where is Ashdod?

This Philistine city is near the Mediterranean Sea.

What's it all about?

When the Philistines captured the Ark of God, the people of Ashdod put it in the temple of their god Dagon. The next morning, they found Dagon had fallen on its face. The day after that, things were worse!

What's an important verse about Ashdod?

The statue of Dagon. . .was, lying on the ground again! It had fallen on its face in front of the ark of the LORD. Its head and hands had been broken off. Only the body of the statue was left.
1 SAMUEL 5:4 NIrV

What does that mean to me?

Be brave, because your God beats out all other gods—hands down!

Assyria

Where is Assyria?

Assyria was a country in the area of today's nations of Turkey and Iraq.

What's it all about?

Sennacherib, the king of Assyria, put his armies all around the city of Jerusalem. They were letting no food or water get through to King Hezekiah and his people. God's people were very hungry and thirsty. But Hezekiah came up with an idea!

What's an important verse about Assyria?

The rest of the events in Hezekiah's reign, including the extent of his power and how he built a pool and dug a tunnel to bring water into the city, are recorded.
2 KINGS 20:20 NLT

What does that mean to me?

When you are in a jam, God will either help you find a way out or bring His blessings in.

Athens

Where is Athens?

In today's country of Greece.

What's it all about?

All the latest ideas in books, plays, and beliefs were talked about in Athens. It was a center of great learning. There people worshipped lots of different idols made into statues.

What's an important verse about Athens?

While Paul was waiting for them [Silas and Timothy] in Athens, he was deeply troubled by all the idols he saw everywhere in the city.
ACTS 17:16 NLT

What does that mean to me?

God is not something made by man's hands. He cannot be contained in clay. He is a spirit living inside of you. You can take Him everywhere you go! He's all you need to know!

Babel

Where is Babel?

This was the name of a tower and a city. The tower was built by ancient people in today's Syria after the Flood.

What's it all about?

Many years ago, everyone spoke the same language. The people began building a tower to reach heaven, to make a name for themselves. To bring them down to earth, God decided to stop their building and show them that *He* was the highest power.

What's an important verse about Babel?

So the name of the city was Babel, because there the Lord mixed up the language of the whole earth. The Lord sent the people everywhere over the whole earth.
GENESIS 11:9 NLV

What does that mean to me?

It's more important to make a name for God than for yourself.

Babylon

Where is Babylon?

An ancient kingdom, Babylon was in southern Mesopotamia.

What's it all about?

Babylon destroyed the nation of Judah, including Jerusalem and its temple, and carried the Israelites off to Babylon. That's where Daniel and his friends—Shadrach, Meshach, and Abednego—ended up. Those friends refused to worship the god of Nebuchadnezzar, king of Babylon, were thrown into a furnace, and lived to tell about it. And Daniel lived after being thrown into a den of lions!

What are some important verses about Babylon?

[King Nebuchadnezzar] carried away to Babylon those who had not been killed by the sword.
2 CHRONICLES 36:20 NLV

Nebuchadnezzar said, "Praise be to the God of Shadrach, Meshach, and Abed-nego. He has sent His angel and saved His servants who put their trust in Him."
DANIEL 3:28 NLV

What does that mean to me?

No matter where you go, God is with you. And, if you trust Him, He will always save you!

Bashan

Where is Bashan?

In the southern part of today's Syria.

What's it all about?

When Moses and the Israelites were wandering around in the desert, they came to the fruitful land of Bashan. Its ruler was King Og, a giant whose iron bed was more than 13 feet long and 6 feet wide.

What's an important verse about Bashan?

Og the king of Bashan went out with all his people to battle at Edrei. But the Lord said to Moses, "Do not be afraid of him. For I have given him into your hand."
NUMBERS 21:33–34 NLV

What does that mean to me?

Don't let giants and bullies scare you. God is bigger than any of them.

Beer-Lahai-Roi

Where is Beer-Lahai-Roi?

Between the towns of Kadesh and Bered in Israel.

What's it all about?

Hagar, a slave woman, was pregnant with Abraham's baby.
Abraham's childless wife, Sarah, started treating Hagar
badly, so Hagar ran away. God found her by a spring of
water. He told her to go back home.

What's an important verse about Beer-Lahai-Roi?

She called him "You are the God who sees me." . . . That's
why the well was named Beer Lahai Roi.
GENESIS 16:13–14 NIrV

What does that mean to me?

God will always find you, no matter where you go. So
you might as well stay right where you are. Tell Him your
troubles. Then listen and obey—and all will be well!

Beer-Sheba

Where is Beer-Sheba?

In the Promised Land, southwest of the town Hebron.

What's it all about?

Abraham sent Hagar and their son Ishmael away with some food and water. They wandered in the desert of Beer-Sheba. After Hagar and Ishmael ran out of water, they sat down and cried. God heard them.

What's an important verse about Beer-Sheba?

God opened Hagar's eyes. She saw a well of water. So she went and filled the bottle with water. And she gave the boy a drink.
GENESIS 21:19 NIrV

What does that mean to me?

Always stay close to God. He will open your eyes so you can see all His blessings and have joy—even through your tears.

Bethany

Where is Bethany?

Near Jerusalem.

What's it all about?

Jesus' good friends Mary, Martha, and Lazarus lived in
Bethany. When Lazarus got sick, his sisters sent a message
for Jesus to come to Bethany. By the time He got there,
Lazarus had been dead for four days.

What's an important verse about Bethany?

Jesus arrived in Bethany, the home of Lazarus—the man he
had raised from the dead. A dinner was prepared in Jesus'
honor. Martha served, and Lazarus was among those who
ate with him.
JOHN 12:1–2 NLT

What does that mean to me?

When you are in trouble, ask for Jesus. Then wait patiently.
He'll get to you—in *His* own *good* time!

Bethel

Where is Bethel?

About 11 miles north of Jerusalem.

What's it all about?

Bethel means "house of God." While running from his angry brother, Esau, Jacob stopped to sleep in Bethel. There he had a dream about a ladder reaching from earth into heaven. Angels were going up and down it. God was at the top of the ladder. He promised never to leave Jacob.

What are some important verses about Bethel?

Jacob woke up from his sleep. Then he thought, "The LORD is certainly in this place. And I didn't even know it. . . . This must be the house of God. This is the gate of heaven."
GENESIS 28:16–17 NIrV

Early the next morning Jacob took the stone he had placed under his head. He set it up as a pillar. . . . He named that place Bethel.
GENESIS 28:18–19 NIrV

What does that mean to me?

God is with you wherever you go—even in the most unusual places in heaven, on earth, and in between.

Bethlehem

Where is Bethlehem?

Five miles south of Jerusalem, Israel.

What's it all about?

Bethlehem is a very important city. That's because lots of good things happened there. It's where Ruth and Boaz, the great-grandparents of King David, met. That's where David was born—*and* where God said *Jesus* would be born!

What are some important verses about Bethlehem?

The LORD says, "Bethlehem, you might not be an important town in the nation of Judah. But out of you will come a ruler over Israel for me."
MICAH 5:2 NIrV

Jesus was born in Bethlehem in Judea. This happened while Herod was king of Judea. After Jesus' birth, Wise Men from the east came to Jerusalem.
MATTHEW 2:1 NIrV

What does that mean to me?

God had Jesus' birth, life, and death planned from the very beginning! So don't worry about what happened today or what is going to happen tomorrow. Just trust God. He's got a plan for you, too!

Bethsaida

Where is Bethsaida?

Northeast of the Sea of Galilee.

What's it all about?

Bethsaida means "house of the fisherman." Philip, Andrew, and Peter were from Bethsaida—and were fisherman! These ordinary people became extraordinary followers of a man named Jesus.

What's an important verse about Bethsaida?

The next day Jesus wanted to go to the country of Galilee. He found Philip and said to him, "Follow Me." Philip was from the town of Bethsaida. Andrew and Peter were from this town also.
JOHN 1:43-44 NLV

What does that mean to me?

God uses ordinary people to do extraordinary things. So get ready—God can equip you to do anything!

Caesarea

Where is Caesarea?

On the shore of the Mediterranean Sea, on the plain of Sharon.

What's it all about?

Cornelius, a Roman commander, was faithful to God. When Peter arrived and talked with Cornelius, the Holy Spirit appeared.

What's an important verse about Caesarea?

A man named Cornelius lived in Caesarea. . . . Some Jewish believers had come with Peter. They were amazed because the gift of the Holy Spirit had been poured out even on those who weren't Jews.
ACTS 10:1, 45 NIrV

What does that mean to me?

It doesn't matter if you are rich or poor, live in America or Europe. The power of the Holy Spirit is for anyone who believes. Do you believe?

Cana

Where is Cana?

In Galilee.

What's it all about?

Jesus, His followers, and His mother, Mary, went to a wedding in Cana. When they ran out of wine, Jesus turned some water into wine. And it was better than what they had been drinking before!

What's an important verse about Cana?

This was the first powerful work Jesus did. It was done in Cana of Galilee where He showed His power. His followers put their trust in Him.
JOHN 2:11 NLV

What does that mean to me?

Give all you have to Jesus—then trust Him to make it even better than before!

Canaan

Where is Canaan?

Also known as the Promised Land, it was west of the Jordan River.

What's it all about?

God told Abraham to leave his home and go to a land God would show him. Abraham had no idea where God was taking him, but he trusted God to keep His promise.

What's an important verse about Canaan?

The Lord said to Abram, "Leave your country, your family and your father's house, and go to the land that I will show you." . . . So they came to the land of Canaan.
GENESIS 12:1, 5 NLV

What does that mean to me?

Like Abraham, you, too, can trust God to lead you. Just step out—even though you might not know where you're headed—into His promise!

Capernaum

Where is Capernaum?

Near the Sea of Galilee.

What's it all about?

When Jesus began teaching in Nazareth, where He had grown up, the people did not accept Him. So, He decided to make Capernaum His home. He did many miracles there.

What are some important verses about Capernaum?

Jesus entered Capernaum again. The people heard that he had come home. So many people gathered that there was no room left.
MARK 2:1–2 NIrV

When Jesus entered Capernaum, a Roman commander came to him. . . . "Lord, I am not good enough to have you come into my house. But just say the word, and my servant will be healed."
MATTHEW 8:5, 8 NIrV

What does that mean to me?

Where you have faith, Jesus can do lots of miracles! So if you need help, run to Him. One word from His lips and all will be well!

City of David

Where is the City of David?

In Israel. This city was first called Jebus, then Jerusalem.

What's it all about?

When David became king, he wanted to make Jebus his capital. It was so well protected, he had trouble getting in. Then David found out the town had a water tunnel.

What's an important verse about the City of David?

The people living in the land. . .said to David, "You will not come here." . . . But David took the strong place of Zion, that is, the city of David.
2 SAMUEL 5:6-7 NLV

What does that mean to me?

When things seem impossible in your eyes, remember— they are not impossible with God.

Colosse

Where is Colosse?

In today's country of Turkey.

What's it all about?

While he was in prison, the apostle Paul wrote a letter to the people of the church in Colosse. The people there were listening to false teachers and moving away from Jesus. Paul's letter later became a Bible book called Colossians.

What's an important verse about Colosse?

We are writing to God's holy people in the city of Colosse, who are faithful brothers and sisters in Christ. May God our Father give you grace and peace.
COLOSSIANS 1:2 NLT

What does that mean to me?

Read and learn from the Word of God. Doing so will keep you close to Jesus' truth and God's power and strength.

Corinth

Where is Corinth?

In the Roman area of Achaia, a western part of today's country of Greece.

What's it all about?

The apostle Paul was a missionary. That means he traveled all over, talking about Jesus and setting up churches. One of the places Paul visited was Corinth. Later he wrote this church two letters. Both can be found in the Bible in books called First and Second Corinthians.

What are some important verses about Corinth?

Paul left Athens and went to Corinth. . . . Paul went to see Aquila and Priscilla. They were tentmakers, just as he was. So he stayed and worked with them.
ACTS 18:1–3 NIrV

Many others who lived in Corinth heard Paul. . . . One night the Lord spoke to Paul in a vision. "Don't be afraid," he said. "Keep on speaking. Don't be silent. I am with you."
ACTS 18:8–10 NIrV

What does that mean to me?

God gave Paul, a tentmaker, lots of courage. If you walk God's way, He'll give you courage, too!

Damascus

Where is Damascus?

In the country of Syria.

What's it all about?

Before becoming a Christian, the apostle Paul was called Saul. Saul was going around killing people who were following Jesus—that is, until Jesus stopped him with a bright light and a booming voice!

What's an important verse about Damascus?

On his journey, Saul approached Damascus. Suddenly a light from heaven flashed around him. He fell to the ground. He heard a voice speak to him.
ACTS 9:3–4 NIrV

What does that mean to me?

Sometimes God will stop you in your tracks. So keep your eyes and ears open to Him. Then listen carefully. God may be trying to tell you something.

Dead Sea

Where is the Dead Sea?

This lowest place on earth is a really big lake in Israel. It's also called the Salt Sea.

What's it all about?

The Dead Sea is four times saltier than the ocean. It's called the Dead Sea because fish can't live in its salty water. But the prophet Ezekiel had a fishy vision about it.

What's an important verse about the Dead Sea?

"The waters of this stream will make the salty waters of the Dead Sea fresh and pure. There will be swarms of living things wherever the water of this river flows. Fish will abound in the Dead Sea."
EZEKIEL 47:8-9 NLT

What does that mean to me?

If you need a fresh start, go to God. He'll help you feel like new!

Derbe

Where is Derbe?

Derbe was in an area called Galatia, which is in today's country of Turkey.

What's it all about?

The apostle Paul stopped here last on his first missionary trip, and first on his second journey.

What's an important verse about Derbe?

Some Jews. . .turned the minds of the people against Paul and Barnabas and told them to throw stones at Paul. . . . They dragged him out of the city thinking he was dead. As the Christians gathered around Paul, he got up and went back into the city. The next day he went with Barnabas to Derbe. ACTS 14:19–20 NLV

What does that mean to me?

God wants believers to help other believers get to a safe place. Who can you "gather around" today?

Ebenezer

Where is Ebenezer?

Near Mizpah in Israel.

What's it all about?

Samuel, a prophet of God, told the Israelites that if they worshiped only the Lord, they would win the next battle over the Philistines. So the Israelites put away their strange gods—and won the battle!

What's an important verse about Ebenezer?

Then Samuel took a stone and set it between Mizpah and Shen. He gave it the name Ebenezer, saying, "The Lord has helped us this far."
1 SAMUEL 7:12 NLV

What does that mean to me?

God is the only one true god who can truly help you. So look to Him—and no one else—for every victory!

Eden, Garden of

Where is the Garden of Eden?

Somewhere along the Tigris and Euphrates rivers in Mesopotamia.

What's it all about?

God put the first two humans—Adam and Eve—in a wonderful garden where they could live in peace and talk with Him every day. But then a snake tempted Adam and Eve to disobey God. So He sent them out of Eden for good.

What's an important verse about the Garden of Eden?

Eve was fooled by the snake in the garden of Eden. In the same way, I am afraid that you will be fooled and led away from your pure love for Christ.
2 CORINTHIANS 11:3 NLV

What does that mean to me?

Don't let anyone fool you into turning away from Jesus. Sticking with Him is your only chance at paradise.

Egypt

Where is Egypt?

On the northern tip of the continent of Africa.

What's it all about?

Sometimes during days of no rain, God's people went to Egypt for food and water. Israel's son Joseph became a powerful leader there. But after he died, the Egyptians made the Israelites their slaves.

What's an important verse about Egypt?

The Lord said [to Moses from a burning bush], "I have seen the suffering of My people in Egypt. I have heard their cry. . . . I know how they suffer. So I have come down to save them."
EXODUS 3:7–8 NLV

What does that mean to me?

God knows what is happening in your life. He hears your cries. He will save you!

Elah Valley

Where is the Elah Valley?

About 15 miles from Bethlehem, Israel.

What's it all about?

In the Elah Valley, King Saul and his soldiers, including the older brothers of a shepherd boy named David, were being teased by a Philistine giant named Goliath. David bravely faced this giant with a simple slingshot and five smooth stones.

What's an important verse about the Elah Valley?

The religious leader said, "The sword is here that belonged to Goliath the Philistine, whom you killed in the valley of Elah." . . . And David said, "There is none like it. Give it to me."
1 SAMUEL 21:9 NLV

What does that mean to me?

No matter how young you are, God can give you the courage to face giants!

Emmaus

Where is Emmaus?

About seven miles from Jerusalem, Israel.

What's it all about?

After Jesus died on the cross, He was buried. Two of His followers, walking on the road to Emmaus, were sad that He was gone. But then He appeared right next to them. When they realized who He was, He disappeared again!

What's an important verse about Emmaus?

The two from Emmaus told their story of how Jesus had appeared to them as they were walking along the road, and how they had recognized him as he was breaking the bread. And just as they were telling about it, Jesus himself was suddenly standing there among them.
LUKE 24:35–36 NLT

What does that mean to me?

Jesus will always pop up—just when you need Him!

Endor

Where is Endor?

About four miles south of Mount Tabor in Israel.

What's it all about?

King Saul chased all the mediums (people who claim to get advice from the spirits of dead people) out of Israel. But then, facing a really big army, Saul became scared and too impatient to wait for God's guidance. So, through a medium, he sought advice from the dead prophet Samuel, who told Saul *he'd* die the next day—and Saul did!

What's an important verse about Endor?

Saul then said to his advisers, "Find a woman who is a medium, so I can go and ask her what to do." His advisers replied, "There is a medium at Endor."
1 SAMUEL 28:7 NLT

What does that mean to me?

Need some wisdom? Wait for *God's* advice. He always knows best!

En-Gedi

Where is En-Gedi?

This oasis called the "spring of the young goat" is on the western side of the Dead Sea.

What's it all about?

King Saul wanted to kill David. While looking for him in En-Gedi, Saul went into a cave. David turned out to be in there. He could've killed Saul—but he didn't. And God rewarded David for it.

What's an important verse about En-Gedi?

After Saul returned from fighting the Philistines, he was told that David had gone into the wilderness of En-gedi. So Saul. . .went to search for David and his men near the rocks of the wild goats.
1 SAMUEL 24:1–2 NLT

What does that mean to me?

God will reward you when you are kind to people who haven't been kind to you.

Ephesus

Where is Ephesus?

The ruins of this once-great city are in Turkey. The apostle Paul's letter to the church in Ephesus, the book of Ephesians, is in the Bible. Revelation 2 also mentions the church of Ephesus.

What's it all about?

In the name of Jesus, seven sons of Sceva, a chief Jewish priest, were driving demons out of people—until a man with an evil spirit jumped on all seven and left them naked and wounded!

What's an important verse about Ephesus?

All through Ephesus. . .fear descended on the city, and the name of the Lord Jesus was greatly honored. Many who became believers confessed their sinful practices.
ACTS 19:17–18 NLT

What does that mean to me?

Jesus' name is powerful—and only to be used by believers with a clean heart!

Galatia

Where is Galatia?

This Roman region is in today's country of Turkey.

What's it all about?

The apostle Paul and Silas journeyed to Galatia on their first missionary trip. Later, Paul wrote to the believers in Galatia. The letter can be found in the Bible book Galatians.

What's an important verse about Galatia?

Paul and Silas traveled through the area of Phrygia and Galatia, because the Holy Spirit had prevented them from preaching the word in the province of Asia at that time. ACTS 16:6 NLT

What does that mean to me?

Sometimes you need to make sure your plans are the same as God's. So before doing anything, check in with Him. He'll let you know which path to take.

Galilee

Where is Galilee?

In northern Israel. The towns of Nazareth, Capernaum, Bethsaida, and Cana are all in Galilee.

What's it all about?

Jesus, the women who supported Him, and eleven of His disciples—all but Judas Iscariot—were from towns in Galilee. It's also where Jesus did most of His miracles.

What are some important verses about Galilee?

There will be a time in the future when Galilee of the Gentiles. . .will be filled with glory. The people who walk in darkness will see a great light.
ISAIAH 9:1–2 NLT

"Men of Galilee," they said, "why are you standing here staring into heaven? Jesus has been taken from you into heaven, but someday he will return from heaven in the same way you saw him go!"
ACTS 1:10–11 NLT

What does that mean to me?

God wants you to stay in the light of Jesus. You can do that by following His rule to love God, yourself, and everyone around you. So shine on! Jesus will be back soon!

Gath

Where is Gath?

Somewhere along the Mediterranean Sea in Israel.

What's it all about?

Goliath, the giant the scrawny little shepherd boy David killed with one stone, was from Gath.

What's an important verse about Gath?

A mighty hero named Goliath came out of the Philistine camp. He was from Gath. He was more than nine feet tall. He had a bronze helmet on his head. He wore a coat of bronze armor. It weighed 125 pounds. On his legs he wore bronze guards. He carried a bronze javelin on his back. His spear was as big as a weaver's rod. Its iron point weighed 15 pounds.
1 SAMUEL 17:4–7 NIrV

What does that mean to me?

Remember to always count on God's strength—not your own! And giants will fall!

Gaza

Where is Gaza?

In today's Palestine.

What's it all about?

Gaza was a Philistine town. After evil Delilah had strongman Samson's hair cut off, the Philistines took the now-weak man to a prison in Gaza. Later, Samson's hair grew back, his God and strength returned, and by his death many Philistines were killed.

What's an important verse about Gaza?

He did not know that the Lord had left him. The Philistines took hold of him and cut out his eyes. They brought him down to Gaza and tied him with brass chains. Samson was made to grind grain in the prison.
JUDGES 16:20–21 NLV

What does that mean to me?

If you stay close to God, He will stay close to you.

Gethsemane

Where is Gethsemane?

This olive-tree grove is just a little way up the Mount of
Olives in Jerusalem, Israel.

What's it all about?

After they ate the Last Supper, Jesus and His disciples went to the Garden of Gethsemane. He told them to stay awake and watch while He prayed. Jesus knew it was the night before He would be killed.

What's an important verse about Gethsemane?

Jesus came with them to a place called Gethsemane. He said to them, "You sit here while I go over there to pray." He took Peter and the two sons of Zebedee with Him. He began to have much sorrow and a heavy heart. . . . He went on a little farther and got down with His face on the ground. He prayed.
MATTHEW 26:36–37, 39 NLV

What does that mean to me?

When you are troubled, follow Jesus' example. Ask some friends to pray for you—or with you. Then go off by yourself and have a secret talk with God. He'll help you.

Gilead

Where is Gilead?

East of the Jordan River, in today's country of Jordan.

What's it all about?

Jephthah promised to give God something—if God would help him win a battle. Jephthah won the fight—but lost his only daughter, who came out to greet him afterward.

What's an important verse about Gilead?

[Jephthah] passed through Gilead. . . . Jephthah made a promise to the Lord and said, "You give the people of Ammon into my hand. And I will give to the Lord whatever comes out of the doors of my house to meet me."
JUDGES 11:29–31 NLV

What does that mean to me?

You don't need to make deals with God to get Him on your side. He's already there!

Gilgal

Where is Gilgal?

A Hebrew word meaning "circle," Gilgal was a town near Jericho.

What's it all about?

Joshua and the Israelites had to cross the flooding Jordan River to get to Gilgal, then Jericho. God helped them by stopping the water from flowing.

What's an important verse about Gilgal?

Joshua set up at Gilgal the twelve stones they had taken from the Jordan. . . . "Your children will ask their fathers some time in the future, 'What do these stones mean?' Then let your children know that Israel crossed this Jordan on dry ground."
JOSHUA 4:20–22 NLV

What does that mean to me?

Find a way to mark how God blesses your life. Then see how many "stones" you end up with!

Golgotha

Where is Golgotha?

In ancient days, Golgotha was just outside of Jerusalem. Today Golgotha is inside Jerusalem's walls.

What's it all about?

Golgotha is where Jesus was crucified on the cross along with two thieves. It was there that He died for our sins.

What's an important verse about Golgotha?

Carrying the cross by himself, he went to the place called Place of the Skull (in Hebrew, *Golgotha*). There they nailed him to the cross. . . . Jesus knew that his mission was now finished. . . . He said, "It is finished!" Then he bowed his head and released his spirit.
JOHN 19:17–18, 28, 30 NLT

What does that mean to me?

Jesus finished His work on earth by dying on the cross for each one of us—and then rising again. But you are just beginning your work. What will you do for Jesus?

Gomorrah

Where is Gomorrah?

Either near or under the Dead Sea.

What's it all about?

Along with its sister city of Sodom in the valley, Gomorrah was full of people who behaved very badly. The city and all its people were destroyed, except for all of Lot's family. Well, almost all. . .

What's an important verse about Gomorrah?

The LORD sent down burning sulfur. It came down like rain on Sodom and Gomorrah. It came from the LORD out of the sky. He destroyed those cities and the whole valley. . . . But Lot's wife looked back. When she did, she became a pillar made out of salt.
GENESIS 19:24–26 NIrV

What does that mean to me?

When God gets you out of trouble, never look back. Just keep moving forward. . .with Him.

Harod Spring

Where is Harod Spring?

In northern Israel.

What's it all about?

Harod means "trembling." At this spring, God told Gideon he had too many soldiers. So Gideon first got rid of men who were afraid, then those who drank water by putting their mouths in the spring instead of cupping it in their hands. So instead of winning the battle with 32,000 soldiers, Gideon won with 300!

What's an important verse about Harod Spring?

Gideon. . .went as far as the spring of Harod. . . . The LORD said to Gideon, "If I let all of you fight the Midianites, the Israelites will boast to me that they saved themselves by their own strength."
JUDGES 7:1–2 NLT

What does that mean to me?

God is the one who gives you the strength to win!

Heaven

Where is heaven?

Somewhere in the sky.

What's it all about?

After Jesus died, He rose up from the grave. Then He talked to His followers, and He rose up to heaven. That's where He hangs out now with God!

What's an important verse about heaven?

Then I saw a new heaven and a new earth. . . . "Look, God's home is now among his people! He will live with them, and they will be his people. God himself will be with them. He will wipe every tear from their eyes, and there will be no more death or sorrow or crying or pain." REVELATION 21:1, 3–4 NLT

What does that mean to me?

Someday you, as a believer, will live with God in heaven!

Hebron

Where is Hebron?

About 20 miles south of Jerusalem in today's West Bank.

What's it all about?

One day Abraham and his nephew split up. Lot went to the Jordan valley. Abraham went to Hebron.

What's an important verse about Hebron?

"Rise up and walk far and wide upon the land. For I will give it to you." Then Abram moved his tent and came to live among the oaks of Mamre in Hebron. There he built an altar to the Lord.
GENESIS 13:17–18 NLV

What does that mean to me?

God loves grateful people. What can you do today as a way to thank Him for what He's given you?

Hell

Where is hell?

A place of much suffering because God isn't there.

What's it all about?

Jesus tells a story about a rich man who had everything but never gave anything to the beggar Lazarus. When both men died, the rich man went to hell and Lazarus to heaven. Between the two places, there was a very big space.

What's an important verse about hell?

"In hell. . .the rich man called out, 'Father Abraham! Have pity on me! Send Lazarus to dip the tip of his finger in water. Then he can cool my tongue with it. I am in terrible pain in this fire.' "
LUKE 16:23–24 NIrV

What does that mean to me?

Stick close to God on earth and you will be cool with Him in heaven!

Iconium

Where is Iconium?

In today's country of Turkey.

What's it all about?

Paul and Barnabas bravely went to Iconium and preached about Jesus. Afterward, some people decided to attack them. The two followers found out about the plan and ran away to preach in other places.

What's an important verse about Iconium?

Paul and Barnabas went to the Jewish synagogue [in Iconium] and preached with such power that a great number of both Jews and Greeks became believers. . . . And the Lord proved their message was true by giving them power to do miraculous signs.
ACTS 14:1, 3 NLT

What does that mean to me?

When you tell people the truth about God, He backs you up in amazing ways.

Israel

Where is Israel?

In the Middle East, on the eastern shore of the
Mediterranean Sea.

What's it all about?

Jacob, afraid and alone, prayed to God. Then he wrestled a
blessing from a strange man. The man renamed Jacob *Israel*,

which means "struggle with God." Later, Jacob's 12 sons got a part of the Promised Land called Israel.

What are some important verses about Israel?

Jacob said, "I will not let you go unless you bless me.". . . . "Your name will no longer be Jacob," the man told him. "From now on you will be called Israel, because you have fought with God and. . .won."
GENESIS 32:26, 28 NLT

"I will give you the land I once gave to Abraham and Isaac. Yes, I will give it to you and your descendants after you."
GENESIS 35:12 NLT

What does that mean to me?

No matter what fix you are in, pray to God. And hold on until He blesses you!

Jabbok River

Where is the Jabbok River?

Near Amman, the capital of today's country of Jordan.

What's it all about?

Some angels greeted Jacob when he neared the Jabbok River. So he camped there. Later he sent many animals across the Jabbok River. They were gifts he hoped would take the sting out of his brother Esau's anger. Later he wrestled with God—and won!

What's an important verse about the Jabbok River?

That night Jacob. . .took his two wives, his two female servants and his 11 sons and sent them across the Jabbok River. After they had crossed the stream, he sent over everything he owned.
GENESIS 32:22–23 NIrV

What does that mean to me?

Sometimes you need to empty your hands to get a good grip on God.

Jericho

Where is Jericho?

On the west side of the Jordan River.

What's it all about?

This is the first city Joshua and the Israelites won in battle as they went in to conquer the Promised Land. They marched around the city for six days. On the seventh, they shouted and Jericho's walls came down!

What's an important verse about Jericho?

The LORD said to Joshua, "I have given you Jericho, its king, and all its strong warriors. You and your fighting men should march around the town."
JOSHUA 6:2–3 NLT

What does that mean to me?

God has battles won before you even begin to fight! Sounds confusing—but it's true! So be brave. With God, anything can happen!

Jerusalem

Where is Jerusalem?

Once called Jebus and the City of David, this hilltop town is in Israel.

What's it all about?

David conquered Jerusalem and made it his capital. This is where David's son Solomon built God's temple, Jesus died on the cross, and His disciples received the Holy Spirit! Jerusalem has been conquered many times and destroyed at least five times.

What are some important verses about Jerusalem?

Pray for peace in Jerusalem. O Jerusalem, may there be peace within your walls and prosperity in your palaces.
PSALM 122: 6–7 NLT

[Jesus said,] "Do not leave Jerusalem until the Father sends you the gift he promised, as I told you before. . . . In just a few days you will be baptized with the Holy Spirit."
ACTS 1:4–5 NLT

What does that mean to me?

World peace begins with you, right where you are. So be a child of peace. Ask Jesus and the Holy Spirit to help you.

Jezreel Valley

Where is the Jezreel Valley?

In northern Israel.

What's it all about?

Many battles were fought in the Jezreel Valley. The Philistines gathered here to fight King Saul, his sons, and their army. Even though Saul had once tried to kill him, King David wrote a song of sadness about Saul and his son Jonathan dying in the Jezreel Valley.

What's an important verse about the Jezreel Valley?

When the Israelites on the other side of the Jezreel Valley and beyond the Jordan saw that the Israelite army had fled and that Saul and his sons were dead, they abandoned their towns and fled. So the Philistines moved in and occupied their towns.
1 SAMUEL 31:7 NLT

What does that mean to me?

God wants us all to be forgiving. . .like David was toward Saul.

Joppa

Where is Joppa?

About 35 miles from Jerusalem. Today Joppa is the city called Jaffa.

What's it all about?

A believer named Tabitha (or Dorcas) lived in Joppa. She was a very good and kind woman who made clothes for others. When she got sick and died, her friends asked Peter to come right away. Peter came, prayed, then told Tabitha to get up. And she did!

What's an important verse about Joppa?

He gave her to them, a living person. News of this went through all Joppa. Many people put their trust in the Lord. ACTS 9:41–42 NLV

What does that mean to me?

God does amazing things for good and kind people. Who can you be kind to today?

Jordan River

Where is the Jordan River?

In Israel.

What's it all about?

Naaman the leper was a captain in the Syrian army. The prophet Elisha in Israel told him what to do to be healed.

Eight hundred years later, Jesus was baptized in the Jordan River, right before defeating the devil in the desert.

What are some important verse about the Jordan

Naaman went down into the Jordan River seven times, as the man of God had told him. And his flesh was made as well as the flesh of a little child. . . . "Now I know that there is no God in all the earth but in Israel."
2 KINGS 5:14–15 NLV

Jesus was full of the Holy Spirit when He returned from the Jordan River. Then He was led by the Holy Spirit to a desert.
LUKE 4:1 NLV

What does that mean to me?

Rivers are wonderful to take a dip in. But your real power comes from God's Holy Spirit! So why not take a dip in God's Word and be led by the Spirit today?

Judah

Where is Judah?

Judah was at first part of the country of Israel. But then the tribes of Israel had a disagreement. So they split. Judah became one country and Israel another. Today Judah is part of southern Israel.

What's it all about?

The country of Judah was named after a son of Jacob (who was later named Israel). It was in Judah that King David and Jesus, members of the tribe of Judah, were born.

What's an important verse about Judah?

God said to him, "Speak to Solomon's son Rehoboam, the king of Judah. Speak to the royal house of Judah and Benjamin. Also speak to the rest of the people. Tell all of them, 'The LORD says, "Do not go up to fight against the Israelites. They are your relatives. I want every one of you to go back home. Things have happened exactly the way I planned them." ' "
1 KINGS 12:22–24 NIrV

What does that mean to me?

No matter who splits from or argues with whom, be at peace. God has a plan!

Kadesh-Barnea

Where is Kadesh-Barnea?

About 90 miles south of Jerusalem, Israel.

What's it all about?

Moses sent 12 tribesmen to scope out Canaan. When they got back, all but Caleb and Joshua scared the people with tales of giants. And all but Caleb and Joshua died during the 40 years of desert wandering.

What's an important verse about Kadesh-Barnea?

Caleb. . .said. . ."I was forty years old when the Lord's servant Moses sent me from Kadesh-barnea to spy out the land. . . . My brothers who went up with me made the heart of the people weak with fear. But I followed the Lord my God with all my heart."
JOSHUA 14:6–8 NLV

What does that mean to me?

Don't follow fear—follow God with all your heart!

Kishon River

Where is the Kishon River?

In the Jezreel Valley in Israel.

What's it all about?

Deborah led the Israelite troops and their army commander, Barak, against attacks by an enemy king and his 900 charioteers. She helped Barak be brave by telling him God was going to hand the charioteers over to him. That's when sudden rain turned the dry Kishon riverbed into a fast-flowing river and swept away or trapped the charioteers in mud.

What's an important verse about the Kishon River?

Barak chased Sisera's chariots and army. . . . All of Sisera's men were killed with swords. Not even one was left.
JUDGES 4:16 NIrV

What does that mean to me?

Stick with God's people. They—and God—will give you courage.

Laodicea

Where is Laodicea?

In today's western Turkey.

What's it all about?

In the Bible book of Revelation, Jesus told the church in Laodicea that its members were neither hot nor cold for Him, so He was going to spit them out of His mouth.

What's an important verse about Laodicea?

"Here I am! I stand at the door and knock. If any of you hears my voice and opens the door, I will come in and eat with you. And you will eat with me."
REVELATION 3:20 NIrV

What does that mean to me?

When you are hot for Jesus and open the door to let Him in, His presence will shine even brighter in you!

Malta

Where is Malta?

In the Mediterranean Sea, south of Italy.

What's it all about?

The prisoner Paul was being taken by ship to Rome to stand trial when the ship ran into a very large storm. The ship wrecked on the island of Malta where Paul got bitten by a poisonous snake—and lived. Later, Paul healed the Maltese leader and other islanders.

What's an important verse about Malta?

Once we were safe on shore, we learned that we were on the island of Malta. The people of the island were very kind to us.
ACTS 28:1-2 NLT

What does that mean to me?

Good things happen when you are kind to others—even when you are having troubles of your own.

Marah

Where is Marah?

In the wilderness of Etham, which was somewhere in northeastern Egypt.

What's it all about?

Three days after Moses led God's people through the Rea Sea, they stopped at Marah. They were very thirsty but couldn't drink the water. After crying out to God, Moses was shown a piece of wood. He threw it into the water and God made it okay to drink!

What's an important verse about Marah?

When they came to the oasis of Marah, the water was too bitter to drink. So they called the place Marah (which means "bitter").
EXODUS 15:23 NLT

What does that mean to me?

When you trust in God as your one and only master and miracle-maker, everything in life becomes sweet.

Midian

Where is Midian?

Some people think it's in Saudi Arabia.

What's it all about?

After killing an Egyptian for beating a Hebrew slave, Moses ran off to Midian. There he met his wife, shepherded sheep, and talked to God in a burning bush. Later, Moses led God's people out of Egypt.

What's an important verse about Midian?

Before Moses left Midian, the LORD said to him, "Return to Egypt, for all those who wanted to kill you have died." So Moses. . .headed back to the land of Egypt. In his hand he carried the staff of God.
EXODUS 4:19–20 NLT

What does that mean to me?

God will give you everything you need to serve Him.

Moab

Where is Moab?

In today's country of Jordan.

What's it all about?

Moab, the son of Lot, and Lot's oldest daughter settled east of Israel. These Moabites became enemies of Israel. Many years later, Naomi, her husband, and her two sons moved to Moab because of a drought. Later, back in Israel, Naomi's widowed daughter-in-law Ruth married Boaz. They had a son named Obed, who became the grandfather of King David.

What's an important verse about Moab?

Naomi returned. And her daughter-in-law Ruth, the Moabite woman, returned with her from the land of Moab. They came to Bethlehem.
RUTH 1:22 NLV

What does that mean to me?

God can use anything and anyone—even a drought, death, and a so-called enemy—to make good things happen!

Mount Carmel

Where is Mount Carmel?

In northern Israel.

What's it all about?

Elijah had a contest with priests who followed a false god that must have been traveling or asleep—because it didn't respond to the priests' prayers. But the one true God proved Himself by answering Elijah's prayer with fire.

What's an important verse about Mount Carmel?

Men who speak for the false gods [were] together at Mount Carmel. Elijah came near all the people and said, "How long will you be divided between two ways of thinking? If the Lord is God, follow Him. But if Baal is God, then follow him."
1 KINGS 18:20–21 NLV

What does that mean to me?

Follow God with your whole heart. Know that He's always around and awake, working things out for you.

Mount Nebo

Where is Mount Nebo?

East of the Jordan River in today's country of Jordan.

What's it all about?

Moses had led God's people to the Promised Land. When they got there, Moses went up Mount Nebo and God showed him the land. Then Moses got to go even higher—to heaven with God!

What's an important verse about Mount Nebo?

Moses went up from the valleys of Moab to Mount Nebo . . . . And the Lord showed him all the land. . . . Moses the servant of the Lord died. . . . And He buried him.
DEUTERONOMY 34:1, 5-6 NLV

What does that mean to me?

The nearer you get to God, the closer you'll get to heaven—in this life and the next!

Mount of Beatitudes

Where is the Mount of Beatitudes?

Somewhere in Israel.

What's it all about?

On the Mount of Beatitudes, Jesus taught the people how they should "be" to be blessed or happy. The word *beatitudes*, which does not show up in the Bible, comes from the Latin word *beatitudo*, which means "blessedness."

What's an important verse about the Mount of Beatitudes?

Jesus went up on the mountainside and sat down. His disciples gathered around him, and he began to teach them. "God blesses those who are. . ."
MATTHEW 5:1–3 NLT

What does that mean to me?

When you follow Jesus' beatitudes (listed in Matthew 5:3–11), you will be a happy dude with a good attitude!

Mount of Olives

Where is the Mount of Olives?

One mile from Jerusalem in Israel.

What's it all about?

Jesus often spent time on the Mount of Olives, alone with God. That gave Jesus the energy to come down the hillside to heal, teach, and preach to the people. It's also the place where He prayed before being arrested—and where He rose to heaven.

Each day Jesus taught at the temple. And each evening he went to spend the night on the hill called the Mount of Olives.
LUKE 21:37 NIrV

"Men of Galilee," they said, "why do you stand here looking at the sky? Jesus has been taken away from you into heaven. But he will come back in the same way you saw him go." The apostles returned to Jerusalem from the Mount of Olives.
ACTS 1:11–12 NIrV

What does that mean to me?

When you spend time alone with God, He will give you the power to do anything—and everything!

Mount Sinai (or Horeb)

Where is Mount Sinai?

Probably on Egypt's Sinai Peninsula.

What's it all about?

Mount Sinai is the place where God met with people.
He met Moses there two times. The first time, Moses was
shepherding his sheep at the mountain's bottom. The

second time, he was shepherding people and met God at the mountaintop.

What are some important verses about Mount Sinai?

He led the flock to the west side of the desert, and came to Horeb, the mountain of God. There the Angel of the Lord showed Himself to Moses in a burning fire from inside a bush.
EXODUS 3:1–2 NLV

The LORD finished speaking to Moses on Mount Sinai. Then he gave him the two tablets of the covenant. They were made out of stone. The words on them were written by the finger of God.
EXODUS 31:18 NIrV

What does that mean to me?

God will always find a way to get a message to His people. Are your eyes and ears open?

Nazareth

Where is Nazareth?

In Galilee, in today's Israel.

What's it all about?

Nazareth was Jesus' hometown. Because the people there only knew Him as the son of Joseph the carpenter, they turned away from the grown-up Jesus who came to preach, teach, and heal others. After He went to heaven, people on earth healed others in His name.

Jesus left there and went to his hometown of Nazareth . . . . Jesus laid his hands on a few sick people and healed them. But he could not do any other miracles there. He was amazed because they had no faith.
MARK 6:1, 5–6 NIrV

Peter said, "I don't have any silver or gold. But I'll give you what I have. In the name of Jesus Christ of Nazareth, get up and walk."
ACTS 3:6 NIrV

To see powerful miracles being done in Jesus' name, you have to believe He is more than just a man from Nazareth. He is God's Son.

New Jerusalem

Where is the New Jerusalem?

Some think it is heaven. Others say it's truly going to be a city that comes down from heaven.

What's it all about?

The Bible book Revelation says that God's people will one day live in a New Jerusalem. It will have streets of gold, where there will be no more pain or sorrow.

What's an important verse about the New Jerusalem?

And I saw the holy city, the new Jerusalem, coming down from God out of heaven.
REVELATION 21:2 NLT

What does that mean to me?

It doesn't really matter if the New Jerusalem is heaven or an actual new place on earth. What matters is that you, as a believer, will get to see it!

Nineveh

Where is Nineveh?

Near today's city of Mosul, Iraq.

What's it all about?

God told the prophet Jonah to go to the people of Nineveh and tell them their city was going to be destroyed. But Jonah didn't think the people would like that message. So he went the other way. After Jonah spent some time in the belly of a big fish, God asked him to go to Nineveh again.

What's an important verse about Nineveh?

This time Jonah obeyed the LORD's command and went to Nineveh, a city so large that it took three days to see it all. JONAH 3:3 NLT

What does that mean to me?

It's always better to obey God—it keeps you from having a whale of a bad time!

Ophrah

Where is Ophrah?

In central Israel.

What's it all about?

A man named Gideon lived in Ophrah. Before he had even thought about becoming a warrior for God, an angel told him, "The Lord is with you, O powerful soldier" (Judges 6:12 NLV).

What's an important verse about Ophrah?

The Lord said to him, "Peace be with you. Do not be afraid. You will not die." Then Gideon built an altar there to the Lord. He gave it the name, The Lord is Peace. It is still in Ophrah.
JUDGES 6:23–24 NLV

What does that mean to me?

Never worry about who you will be. Just worship God—and He'll give you the strength to be that special person He knows you already are!

Paradise

Where is Paradise?

In God's perfect garden.

What's it all about?

Adam and Eve lived in a wonderful garden. There was no evil or death in it. Every day they walked and talked with God. But when they disobeyed God, they were sent out of Paradise.

What's an important verse about Paradise?

"Anyone with ears to hear must listen to the Spirit and understand what he is saying to the churches. To everyone who is victorious I will give fruit from the tree of life in the paradise of God."
REVELATION 2:7 NLT

What does that mean to me?

If you stick with Jesus and walk like He walked, you will someday be with God in Paradise!

Patmos

Where is Patmos?

Off the coast of today's country of Turkey.

What's it all about?

As punishment for talking to people about Jesus, John was sent away to the small island of Patmos. There he had a vision. He wrote down everything he saw. It is in the Bible book called Revelation.

What's an important verse about Patmos?

I, John, am a believer like you. I am a friend who suffers like you. As members of Jesus' royal family, we can put up with anything that happens to us. I was on the island of Patmos because I taught God's word and what Jesus said.
REVELATION 1:9 NIrV

What does that mean to me?

With Jesus, God's royal Son, as your Friend and Brother, you can get through anything!

Pergamum

Where is Pergamum?

In today's western Turkey.

What's it all about?

In the Bible book Revelation, Jesus had some words to say to seven churches. One of those seven was in Pergamum. Members of that church were following teachers who were leading them into doing wrong things.

What's an important verse about Pergamum?

"Here is what I command you to write to the church in Pergamum. . . . 'I have a few things against you. You have people there who follow the teaching of Balaam.'" REVELATION 2:12, 14 NIrV

What does that mean to me?

God wants you—and everyone at your church—to be following His teachings only. Then you will be doing the right things.

Persia

Where is Persia?

In today's country of Iran.

What's it all about?

At one time, Cyrus, a powerful ruler from Persia, defeated the country of Babylon and freed the Jewish people who had been sent there.

What's an important verse about Persia?

This is what King Cyrus of Persia says: "The LORD, the God of heaven, has given me all the kingdoms of the earth. He has appointed me to build him a Temple at Jerusalem, which is in Judah. Any of you who are the LORD's people may go there for this task. And may the LORD your God be with you!"

2 CHRONICLES 36:23 NLT

What does that mean to me?

God can get anyone—even one's so-called enemies—to do His work.

Philadelphia

Where is Philadelphia?

In today's western Turkey.

What's it all about?

In the Bible book of Revelation, Jesus had some words for seven churches, Philadelphia being one of them. Because its members were great followers, He said others would know "that you are the ones I love" (Revelation 3:9 NLT).

What's an important verse about Philadelphia?

"Write this letter to the angel of the church in Philadelphia . . . . I know all the things you do, and I have opened a door for you that no one can close. You have little strength, yet you obeyed my word and did not deny me."
REVELATION 3:7–8 NLT

What does that mean to me?

Are you following God as much as your strength allows? If so, look for doors He is opening for you!

Philippi

Where is Philippi?

In today's country of Greece.

What's it all about?

Lydia lived in Philippi. She invited the apostle Paul to start a church in her home, which became the first church in Europe.

What's an important verse about Philippi?

We traveled to Philippi, a Roman colony. . . . One of those listening was a woman named Lydia. She was from the city of Thyatira. Her business was selling purple cloth. She was a worshiper of God. The Lord opened her heart to accept Paul's message.
ACTS 16:12, 14 NIrV

What does that mean to me?

Your job is to tell people about God's love. It's His job to open their hearts to receive the wonders of it.

Red Sea

Where is the Red Sea?

Between the continents of Africa and Arabia.

What's it all about?

After Egypt went through ten plagues, its pharaoh finally agreed to free the Jewish slaves. But then he changed his mind. Pharaoh and his army chased after the Israelites, following them into the Red Sea—where he and his army drowned.

What's an important verse about the Red Sea?

Then Moses reached his hand out over the Red Sea. All that night the LORD pushed the sea back with a strong east wind. He turned the sea into dry land. The waters were parted.
EXODUS 14:21–22 NIrV

What does that mean to me?

If God is powerful enough to push back the sea, He's powerful enough to rescue you from anything and anyone.

Rome

Where is Rome?

In Italy.

What's it all about?

The apostle Paul was arrested during a riot in Jerusalem.
Then he had to travel to Rome to be tried in a court there.

While in prison in Rome, Paul ended up telling many people about God.

What are some important verses about Rome?

That night the Lord appeared to Paul and said, "Be encouraged, Paul. Just as you have been a witness to me here in Jerusalem, you must preach the Good News in Rome as well."
ACTS 23:11 NLT

For the next two years, Paul lived in Rome at his own expense. He welcomed all who visited him, boldly proclaiming the Kingdom of God and teaching about the Lord Jesus Christ. And no one tried to stop him.
ACTS 28:30–31 NLT

What does that mean to me?

God has a plan for your life, so don't worry about what's happening—or not happening. And don't worry about where you are, because God will always put you right where He needs you.

Samaria

Where is Samaria?

In Israel.

What's it all about?

In Jesus' day, Jews hated people from Samaria. That's why His Jewish listeners didn't like His story about how two of their worship leaders walked right by an injured man lying on the road. Even worse, it was a dreaded Samaritan who *did* help the man and proved himself a wonderful neighbor.

What's an important verse about Samaria?

"Going over to him, the Samaritan soothed his wounds with olive oil and wine and bandaged them. Then he put the man on his own donkey and took him to an inn, where he took care of him."
LUKE 10:34 NLT

What does that mean to me?

Being a good neighbor means showing kindness to everyone—no matter who they (or you) are!

Sardis

Where is Sardis?

In today's country of Turkey.

What's it all about?

In Revelation, the last book of the Bible, Jesus had some words for seven churches—Sardis was one of them.

What's an important verse about Sardis?

"Here is what I command you to write to the church in Sardis. . . . 'Remember what you have been taught and have heard. Obey it. Turn away from your sins.'"
REVELATION 3:1, 3 NIrv

What does that mean to me?

To be a true follower of Jesus, you must not just read His Word (the Bible) but also do what it says. Then you will win over evil—and be good with God!

Sea of Galilee

Where is the Sea of Galilee?

In Israel.

What's it all about?

The Sea of Galilee is really a lake. Here Jesus first met some of His fishermen disciples and walked on water.

What are some important verses about the Sea of Galilee?

Jesus made the disciples get into the boat. He had them go on ahead of him to the other side of the Sea of Galilee. . . . Peter got out of the boat. He walked on the water toward Jesus. But when Peter saw the wind, he was afraid. He began to sink.
MATTHEW 14:22, 29–30 NIrV

One day Jesus said to his disciples, "Let's cross to the other side of the lake." . . . When Jesus woke up, he rebuked the wind and the raging waves. Suddenly the storm stopped and all was calm.
LUKE 8:22, 24 NLT

What does that mean to me?

With your eyes on Jesus, you can do anything. And with Him in your boat, you need not fear any storms!

Shiloh

Where is Shiloh?

North of Jerusalem, Israel.

What's it all about?

Shiloh was where Joshua divided up the Promised Land and set up the tent of the tabernacle of God. Later in

Shiloh, Hannah prayed for a son from God—and got one. Later the Philistines stole the Ark from Shiloh and the town was destroyed.

What are some important verses about Shiloh?

Once after a sacrificial meal at Shiloh, Hannah got up and went to pray [for a son]. . . . When the child was weaned, Hannah took him to the Tabernacle in Shiloh. . . . The LORD continued to appear at Shiloh and gave messages to Samuel there.
1 SAMUEL 1:9, 24; 3:21 NLT

"Go now to the place at Shiloh where I once put the Tabernacle that bore my name. See what I did there because of all the wickedness of my people, the Israelites. . . . I destroyed Shiloh."
JEREMIAH 7:12, 14 NLT

What does that mean to me?

God lifts up the good and brings down the evil.

Shunem

Where is Shunem?

In Israel, south of Nazareth.

What's it all about?

A wealthy woman in Shunem was nice to God's prophet Elisha. In return for her kindness, he promised God would give her a son. And God did! Later, when that son died, Elisha brought him back to life.

What's an important verse about Shunem?

One day Elisha went to the town of Shunem. A wealthy woman lived there, and she urged him to come to her home for a meal. After that, whenever he passed that way, he would stop there for something to eat.
2 KINGS 4:8 NLT

What does that mean to me?

When you are kind to God's people, God shines His favor on you!

Siloam Pool

Where is the Siloam Pool?

Inside the walls of Jerusalem, Israel.

What's it all about?

King Hezekiah's workers built a tunnel from the spring outside Jerusalem's walls to what was named the Siloam Pool, which was right inside the city walls. Hundreds of years later, Jesus sent a blind man to that pool to wash his eyes.

What's an important verse about the Siloam Pool?

[Jesus] spit on the ground. He made some mud with the spit. Then he put the mud on the man's eyes. "Go," he told him. "Wash in the Pool of Siloam." Siloam means Sent. So the man went and washed. And he came home able to see.
JOHN 9:6-7 NIrV

What does that mean to me?

If you have a problem, go to Jesus. He'll open your eyes.

Smyrna

Where is Smyrna?

In today's country of Turkey.

What's it all about?

In Revelation, the last book of the Bible, Jesus had some words for seven churches—Smyrna was one of them. He had nothing but good things to say about members of that church! Because they were great followers who suffered, He promised them eternal life.

What's an important verse about Smyrna?

"Here is what I command you to write to the church in Smyrna. . . . 'I know that you suffer and are poor. But you are rich!' "
REVELATION 2:8–9 NIrV

What does that mean to me?

Having Jesus in your life is better than anything on earth—even gold! He is your true treasure.

Sodom

Where is Sodom?

Either near or under the Dead Sea.

What's it all about?

Along with its sister city of Gomorrah, Sodom was full of people who behaved very badly. Because Abraham asked God to spare any godly people in the cities, the Lord sent angels to rescue Abraham's nephew Lot.

What's an important verse about Sodom?

[Abraham] looked down toward Sodom and Gomorrah and the whole valley. . . . When God destroyed the cities of the valley, he showed concern for Abraham. He brought Lot out safely when he destroyed the cities where Lot had lived. GENESIS 19:28–29 NIrV

What does that mean to me?

God listens to your prayers and rescues those you love. Who can you pray for today?

Sychar

Where is Sychar?

In Samaria.

What's it all about?

Jesus stopped to rest at a well in Sychar. There He met a woman. He told her many things about herself—and that her spirit would never thirst with Him, the living water, in her life. After their talk, she went and told others that He must be the Christ, the one who would save them all.

What's an important verse about Sychar?

Many of the Samaritans from the town of Sychar believed in Jesus. They believed because of the woman's witness. She said, "He told me everything I've ever done."
JOHN 4:39 NIrV

What does that mean to me?

Jesus knows everything about you. So trust Him with your life—and drink in His never-ending love!

Tarshish

Where is Tarshish?

Somewhere west of Israel.

What's it all about?

God told Jonah to tell the evil people in Nineveh that God was going to destroy their town. But Jonah didn't obey Him. Jonah went the other way and ended up in the belly of a huge fish. Later he *did* go to Nineveh after all.

What's an important verse about Tarshish?

Jonah. . .went down to Joppa and found a ship which was going to Tarshish. Jonah paid money, and got on the ship to go with them, to get away from the Lord.
JONAH 1:3 NLV

What does that mean to me?

No matter where you go, God will always find a way to turn you back around to doing what *He* thinks is best.

Thessalonica

Where is Thessalonica?

In today's country of Greece.

What's it all about?

Paul and his friends went to Thessalonica to tell its people about Jesus. The Thessalonians joyfully followed the example of these Christian workers.

What's an important verse about Thessalonica?

We are sending this letter to you, the members of the church in Thessalonica. . . . You welcomed our message with the joy the Holy Spirit gives. So you became a model to all the believers in the lands of Macedonia and Achaia. 1 THESSALONIANS 1:1, 6–7 NIrV

What does that mean to me?

Do your best to be like Jesus. And before you know it, others will be following your example.

Thyatira

Where is Thyatira?

In today's country of Turkey.

What's it all about?

In Revelation, the last book of the Bible, Jesus had some words for seven churches—Thyatira was one of them. Even though some of its people were remaining faithful to Jesus, some were listening to Jezebel, an evil teacher in their church.

What's an important verse about Thyatira?

"Write this to the angel of the church in the city of Thyatira. . . . 'You are allowing Jezebel who calls herself a preacher to teach my servants. She is leading them in the wrong way.'"
REVELATION 2:18, 20 NLV

What does that mean to me?

To stay on the right track, follow the words of Jesus. He will teach you all the right ways to live.

Troas

Where is Troas?

In today's country of Turkey.

What's it all about?

In Troas, Paul was preaching late into the night. As Paul talked and talked, the young man Eutychus was sitting on a windowsill. He ended up not only falling asleep but falling out the window!

What's an important verse about Troas?

[Eutychus] fell sound asleep and dropped three stories to his death below. Paul went down, bent over him, and took him into his arms. "Don't worry," he said, "he's alive!" . . . Meanwhile, the young man was taken home alive and well, and everyone was greatly relieved.
Acts 20:9–10, 12 NLT

What does that mean to me?

Make sure you keep your ears—and eyes—wide open to the Word of God!

Ur

Where is Ur?

In today's country of Iraq.

What's it all about?

Abraham was born and brought up in Ur and later moved to Haran. Then God told him to go to a land God would show him. And the faithful Abraham left.

What's an important verse about Ur?

"You are the LORD God, who chose Abram and brought him from Ur of the Chaldeans and renamed him Abraham. When he had proved himself faithful, you made a covenant with him. . . . And you have done what you promised, for you are always true to your word."
NEHEMIAH 9:7–8 NLT

What does that mean to me?

God always keeps His promises—no matter where you go or where He sends you.

Uz

Where is Uz?

Somewhere in the Middle East—no one knows for sure.

What's it all about?

Job, a man of God, was rich in faith, family, animals, wealth, and health. First the devil took his stuff—including his family. Then he attacked Job's body. But because Job never cursed God, he gained more in the end than he had in the beginning of his story.

What's an important verse about Uz?

There was a man who lived in the land of Uz. His name was Job. He was honest. He did what was right. He had respect for God and avoided evil.
JOB 1:1 NIrV

What does that mean to me?

When, no matter what, you stick things out with God, you will be even more blessed!

Zarephath

Where is Zarephath?

In today's country of Lebanon.

What's it all about?

God sent Elijah to a widow in Zarephath for food. But she had no bread—only a little flour and oil. So Elijah told her to make some bread with what little she did have, and God would make sure she had enough.

What's an important verse about Zarephath?

Elijah had food every day. There was also food for the woman and her family. The jar of flour wasn't used up. The jug always had oil in it. That's what the LORD had said would happen.
1 KINGS 17:15–16 NIrV

What does that mean to me?

God has a way of making a lot out of a little—so use what you have for Him, and you'll have more than enough.